Careers: Radiologist

© 2013 - 2014 A. L. Dawn French
All rights reserved

ISBN-13: 978-1495228322
ISBN-10: 1495228320
This book has been assigned a CreateSpace ISBN.

Online Edition: January 2014

Cover design by the Author
Images used from Clipart

Publisher
    Double F Publishing House
    P O Box 564, Castries
    SAINT LUCIA
    dawnnbooks@gmail.com

    e|i - educational and informative

Health is a state of complete physical, mental, and social well-being andnot merely the absence of disease or infirmity.

World Health Organisation

Available online at http://tiny.cc/dawnnbooks

Table of Contents

FOREWORD 4
INTRODUCTION 5
WHAT IS A RADIOLOGIST? 7
WHAT SUBJECTS DO I NEED? 7
    EXTRACURRICULAR ACTIVITIES 8
WHAT EDUCATION PATH SHOULD I CONSIDER? 9
HOW DO I FUND MY EDUCATION? 13
    THE RIGHTS OF THE CHILD 13
    PLANNING 13
    THE PRIORITY LIST 14
    SCHOLARSHIPS 14
2BINDING CLAUSES 16
    FUNDING YOURSELF 16
HOW DO I FUND MY BUSINESS? 17
THE INTERVIEW 18
WHAT ARE THE WORK OPPORTUNITIES WHEN I GRADUATE? 20
PROFESSIONAL DEVELOPMENT 22
    THE LAW 22
    CONTINUING PROFESSIONAL DEVELOPMENT 22
    PROFESSIONAL ASSOCIATIONS 22
ACKNOWLEDGEMENTS 23
NOTES 24
WHAT THE REVIEWERS ARE SAYING… 26
COMPLIMENTARY INFORMATION 28

Foreword

Many students complete their secondary schooling unsure of the career path they wish to pursue. Still very few complete post-secondary education knowing their chosen career path. Information to guide students on choosing their career paths is not readily available locally. The few career guidance showcases put on by the school system falls short of providing meaningful information for students. The importance of knowing at an early stage the pathway to a chosen career is invaluable as it saves time, worry, anxiety and financial resources.

This is where Dawn French and her Careers series come in. Whether you are a parent, a student or someone looking to a new career, this series provides invaluable information on the common career pathways in Saint Lucia. The information presented is simple to understand and straight to the point. The series provides information on academic qualifications/skills requirements, educational institutions, scholarship/financial aid opportunities, an interview primer and potential employment opportunities.

I encourage everyone interested in pursuing a career to get their hands on a copy of their chosen Career book. This little investment will pay off huge dividends in the long term as it will guide you in pursuing your chosen career.

Laurianus Lesfloris
Corporate Manager

Introduction

This book is part of a series of books with a simple twofold objective:

The first aim is to expose young people to the fact that there are many careers out there. Some that you may not have considered and othersyou may have thought about but have rejected for various reasons. We are here to tell you that once you approach your career choice in a professional, logical and business manner there is no reason why you should not pursue your dream.

The second aim is: Get educated!!!! If you are in school, stay in school. The longer you can stay in school and get a formal education the easier it will be to market yourself. Make no mistake the level of your education: primary, secondary, college or university, will determine the level of the job that you end up with. For example, compare the grades and education standards required within the public service in Saint Lucia:

> Grade 1 in the Government Service (Driver)
> School Leaving Certificate OR
> Post Primary School Leaving Certificate
> No experience is required
>
> Grade 20 in the Government Service (Permanent Secretary)
> Master's Degree plus Advanced Certificate in Administration and Management plus eight years Civil Service experience OR
> Bachelor's Degree plus Certificate in Administration and Management plus ten years Civil Service experience.

Finally, this book like all the others I have written is in plain, ole, simple English so that we can all understand.

So I present you the reader with the age old question.... *What do you want to be when you grow up?*

Let's explore together.

A. L. Dawn French
Architect/Town Planner/Disaster Manager/Author

What is a Radiologist?

A Radiologist is medical doctor and is a specialist who assists other Doctors with their diagnosis by using medical imaging technologies, such as MRI and CT as well as radioactive substances and X-rays.

What subjects do I need?

English and Mathematics are always a must, never more so than for a Radiologist. You will need to be able to calibrate the equipment you will also need to be able to read and write reports.

1. You will need to follow the Science subjects at school. Such as Integrated Science/Biology/ Human and Social Biology/ Agricultural Science or Chemistry as well as have a thorough understanding of anatomy and physiology. If you attend the Centre for Adolescent Renewal and Education (CARE) the school may be able to arrange for you to follow the science classes in partnership with a secondary school. Ask your teacher!

2. ICT: You will need to be competent in the use of computers. A basic overall understanding of computers and programs will be necessary as your field is progressively getting more and more technologically advanced.

3. Principles of Business/Accounts: Ensure you understand the money aspect of your career. It is more than likely that one day you may become a small Business Owner. Learn some of the fundamentals of business at school. There are lots of hidden costs that persons entering careers do not recognize e.g. the importance of having spares for equipment, of insurance of

equipment, loss of income insurance, purchase of computer and license as well as the upgrading of software.

4. <u>Languages:</u> French and Spanish - though not absolutely necessary to your chosen career, a foreign language can be an asset. The ability to speak three languages (this includes English) will give you an advantage over many candidates. The ability to speak three languages will mean that you will truly be able to work anywhere in the world.

Extracurricular activities

1. Accidents can happen at any time, ensure you receive First Aid/CPR Training which is offered by St John (451-6122) and Red Cross (452-5582).

2. Online or old school read one of these:
    a. Clinical Radiology Made Ridiculously Simple by Hugue and M.D. Ouellette
    b. Grant Writing for Dummies by Beverly A. Browning
    c. Small Business for Dummies by Eric Tyson and Jim Schell
    d. Home-Based Business for Dummies by Paul Edwards, Sarah Edwards and Peter Economy
    e. Business Plans for Dummies by Paul Tiffany and Steven D. Peterson
    f. The Saint Lucian Phonetic Dictionary by Malcolm Charles.
    g. A Commonsense Approach to the Job Market by A. L. Dawn French
    h. Works for Me: Sales and Marketing by A. L. Dawn French

3. Join the Junior Achievers Program at your school - **http://lc.unleashingideas.org/users/jaslu** the Junior Achievers Program uses a model of encouraging young people to create and run a business; this is a unique and practical approach to economic education and leadership development. Use your career ambitions as the Business Model. This way in the safety of your school, you can identify the positives and negatives associated with your career choice. You then have a business model to follow when you have completed your studies.

4. Take part in the Ministry of Education's Annual National Schools` Science and Technology Fair

5. As part of a major event a Master Class may be offered. Take part and learn as much as you can from others in your field.

What education path should I consider?

1. If you need to improve your English and Mathematics grades:
    a. UWI Open Campus (Saint Lucia) offers CXC English and Mathematics.
    b. The National Enrichment Learning Program (NELP) offers:
        i. Basic English and Mathematics (Level 1-3)
        ii. Pre CXC English and Mathematics
        iii. CXC English and Mathematics
    c. Borderlais Correctional Facility offers CXC English and Mathematics.

2. Once you have mastered English and Mathematics, you may consider entering the Sir Arthur Lewis Community College Division of Arts, Science and General Studies.

3. You may consider not going to the Community College and attending medical school directly. A comprehensive list of medical schools in the Caribbean can be viewed at **http://en.wikipedia.org/wiki/List_of_medical_schools_in_the_Caribbean**

4. Languages:
    a. The Venezuelan Institute offers Spanish classes
    b. The Alliance Francaise offers French classes
    c. Read the Saint Lucian Phonetic Dictionary by Malcolm Charles.
    d. Consider taking the *Creole Language* course offered by the Harold Simmons Folk Academy. Call the Folk Research Centre for details of the next scheduled course.
    e. Sign up for writing tips at **http://www.dailywritingtips.com/**

5. Follow the general courses offered by
    a. The Centre for Adolescent Renewal and Education (CARE)
    b. NELP
    c. National Research and Development Foundation (NRDF)
    d. Bordelais Correctional Facility

6. **https://www.coursera.org** offers an online course on Public Speaking. The NRDF also offers a course in Effective Speaking. As a Radiologist you will be expected to be able to hold consultation with clients and colleagues. You may even present papers at conferences.

7. The programs at the National Skills Development Centre (NSDC) are project driven and so the subjects offered vary from semester to semester. Call the NSDC at 458-1677 to see what courses are being offered this semester. As a standard, however, Productivity Enhancement Training (PET) is always offered. PET addresses the subject of Life Skills and Human interaction; a valuable skill for any career.

8. ICT Courses are offered by:
    a. National Enrichment Learning Program (NELP)
    b. National Research and Development Foundation (NRDF)
    c. National Skills Development Centre (NSDC)
    d. Sir Arthur Lewis Community College
    e. Bordelais Correctional Facility
    f. Monroe College

If you attend the Centre for Adolescent Renewal and Education (CARE) or are at the Bordelais Correctional Facility (BCF) take the opportunity to acquire the all-round education that is offered.

> It is necessary to know the fundamentals of English e.g. when to use:
> Amount/Number
> Borrow/Lend

If you are a "graduate" of the BCF, confess your record to your place of work from the beginning and assure your Boss that you have been rehabilitated and are now an upstanding citizen. Don't let them find out from someone else.

Once you have completed this phase of your studies you will need to further your education by attending a College or University, the one you choose will depend on you. Below are a few examples of tertiary institutions within the Caribbean region:

1. The UWI Open Campus (Saint Lucia) offers:
   a. ASc in Business Management
   b. Certificate in Entrepreneurship

2. The University of the West Indies offers a Doctor of Medicine Degree in Radiology at
   a. Mona Campus (Jamaica)
   b. St Augustine Campus (Trinidad)

3. University of Guyana offers an Associate Degree in Radiography

4. University of Puerto Rico offers Diagnostic Radiology. A proficiency in Spanish is needed.

5. University of Technology, Jamaica offers a Bachelor of Health Sciences in Radiology

6. Spartan University (Saint Lucia) as part of its medical program offers Radiology.

Volunteer with a Radiologist – yes volunteer, don't ask to be paid for you are there for something more valuable than money – experience. Working with a Radiologist will give you a practical appreciation of the theory that will be presented in your studies. Just as important as the work will be the fact that you can then add this experience to your curriculum vitae (CV) or your résumé when the time comes for you to search for a job.

Contact the Saint Lucia Medical and Dental Association at http://slmda.org/contact/ to inquire regarding a member who may be willing to mentor you.

How do I fund my education?

The Rights of the Child

It is the right of every child to be educated.
It is not the right of every child to get a scholarship.

It is the right of every child to have a dream.
It is the duty of every parent to do all in their power to ensure that that dream becomes a reality.

Planning

Unfortunately we are not a people who plan. We all need to realize that planning for our children's education starts at birth. Whether you come from a family of one child or eight, your parents need to plan for the education of each one of you. Parents must plan for the education of each child with the understanding that it is their duty and no one else's to take care of their children; to feed, to clothe and to educate.

There are many education savings plans available at financial institutions, which can be established at birth for the child. Saving a small amount over 15 – 20 years can yield a substantial savings over the years due to the effect of compound interest.

In the end, your parents may have to face a financial institution and negotiate a student loan for you.

And oh yes... will VAT affect your plans?

The Priority List

Some career paths can be fulfilled because some professions are higher profile than others e.g. Medicine.

Recognizing this, the Government of Saint Lucia has developed a List of Areas for National Training for Student Loans and Economic Cost Awards, better known as the *Priority List*. This list has existed for decades and is reviewed as the needs of the country changes and new opportunities present themselves. No one is guaranteed a scholarship, loan or economic cost.

You may view an example of the Government of Saint Lucia's listing at
http://www.govt.lc/www/text/PriorityList2014.pdf

Scholarships

There are a limited number of scholarships to Secondary School, College and University. Some may be available where your parents work or from Financial Institutions such as Credit Unions.

Ask at your school about the Sir John Compton Memorial Foundation.

If you live in Choiseul you may qualify for the Lusca Theophilus Scholarship Fund. Or the Bernadette Theophilus Scholarship which is intended exclusively for students from Caffiere (Choiseul).

You may also visit the Training Department of the Ministry of the Public Service to ask about available scholarships or visit the website at
http://www.govt.lc/search/scholarships

A number of partners offer funding, such as:
   a. Organisation of American States (OAS)
   b. Caribbean Tourism Organisation (CTO)
   c. Caribbean Hotel Association (CHA)
   d. Caribbean Catastrophe Risk Insurance Facility (CCRIF)
   e. Government of New Zealand
   f. Taiwanese Government

There are a limited number of scholarships available to the youth of the Nation and every year the competition for them intensifies. The number of scholarships is also not as many as they used to be and those available are sometimes not full scholarships. This means that

2013 - The Russian Federation embassy in Jamaica announced they are to provide for talented young people from Saint Lucia; grants for training in federal public educational institutions of higher and secondary professional education at the expense of the Russian federal budget.

your parents may still have to find some money to assist you even if you do get awarded a scholarship.

The job of every parent is to operate on the assumption that their child may not be awarded a scholarship. Not that you are not bright – it's just that there may not be enough scholarships to go around and so alternate funding may have to be investigated.

Binding Clauses

A scholarship is NOT FREE MONEY. The Government is providing funding, through the provision of binding scholarships, for the training of persons who choose to follow a course identified on the Priority List. As the recipient of a scholarship you are required to return to Saint Lucia to work for the period equivalent to the length of time you were on scholarship e.g. if the scholarship is for three years you will be expected to work for a minimum of three years.

The binding clause for a bank loan is different. You are obligated to pay your loan back or the bank will seize the collateral given to guarantee the loan.

Funding Yourself

If all else fails, then fund yourself. This option will take every ounce of discipline and determination that you have. This option will test your patience as it may take years for you to be in the position to go to University. This option means that you will have to get a job, while many of your friends go to University.

But you are worth it. Keep your career goal as your beacon. If you are not willing to find a way to invest in yourself, who will?

Many Financial Intuitions have a Financial Planner, so talk to one. Agree on a strategy, stay with your plan and never let go of your dream.

How do I fund my business?

It is possible that you will start your own business and create your own products. It is important you understand the processes involved.

1. As part of its Loan Facility, BELfund offers a compulsory Business Management Training Course.
   http://www.belfundstlucia.com

2. The Small Enterprise Development Unit (SEDU) in collaboration with the Sir Arthur Lewis Community College (SALCC) offers a range of evening classes for Entrepreneurs.
   http://www.commerce.gov.lc/departments/view/1

3. Saint Lucia Youth Business Trust (SLYBT) offers access to start-up capital, business mentoring, networking, advisory and marketing support services.
   http://www.slybt.org/

BELFund:
451-6069/8858

Saint Lucia Development Bank:
456-7532

Small Enterprise Development Unit:
468-4218/468-4202

Saint Lucia Youth Business Trust:
452-3165

The Interview

Some scholarships require an interview. Prepare for this the way you would for a job. In fact it is a job – the job of STUDENT.

These tips are also valid when you are applying for a job. Further information is available from *"A Commonsense Approach to the Job Market"* By A. L. Dawn French at
http://www.amazon.com/dp/B00BDTUKM0

1. <u>Time:</u> Unfortunately we are not a society that respects time. But to the interviewer – TIME IS MONEY. Be a minimum of 15 minutes early. So if the interview is set for 10:00am arrive for 9:45am for the latest. This way any challenges/problems can be dealt with in a timely manner. Not to mention if you had to walk, then you have the time to cool down, even to use the toilet or to freshen up.

2. <u>Clothes:</u> First impressions last – If you arrive in t-shirt and jeans (below the bum as is the style) it is very likely that you will not get the scholarship.

    Use formal clothes:
    - Dark colours e.g. black & white, blues and browns
    - Knee length skirts or loose trousers and tops with sleeves for girls, not tight skirt/pants/shirt and certainly not jeans.
    - Loose trousers not baggy and shirt with collar and sleeves for boys, and certainly not jeans.

    Use as little "bling" as possible; that means replace the large earrings with studs and if you happen to have five holes in the ear remove all five earrings and leave one conservative one on. This also applies to any other visible body piercings (eyes, nose, tongue etc.) Remove the cow chain from around your neck.

3. Hygiene & Personal Grooming:
    a. Keep your hair style to a conservative and professional design. Regardless of your gender, if you have long hair it is strongly recommended that you keep it tied into a pony tail to the back of your head.
    b. If you must use a cologne/perfume keep it light and not strong/overpowering.
    c. Ensure that tattoos are covered up as much as possible
    d. Reduce on your heavy make-up.

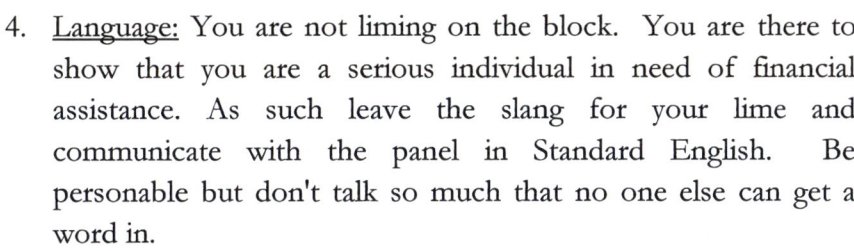

Available online from http://tiny.cc/dawnnboooks & Print-on-Demand from dawnnbooks@gmail.com

4. Language: You are not liming on the block. You are there to show that you are a serious individual in need of financial assistance. As such leave the slang for your lime and communicate with the panel in Standard English. Be personable but don't talk so much that no one else can get a word in.

5. Phones: Turn the cell/BB (BBM &WhatsApp) OFF!

6. Etiquette: This is the polite acknowledgement of the persons in the room with you. "Good day" as you enter and "Thank You"

as you are about to leave make a positive impact on the interview panelists.

What are the work opportunities when I graduate?

Job opportunities depend on where you wish your career to lead you.

1. Locally you may consider working in the Public Service, probably with the Ministry of Health at one of the Hospitals.
   In Saint Lucia there are prescribed forms for Application to the Public Service Commission and the Teaching Service Commission, the forms may be found for download at **http://archive.stlucia.gov.lc/govforms/services_commission_application_forms.htm**

2. It is possible that you will work for yourself by starting your own Practice. Your Practice has the potential to go regional and international.

3. With the freedom of movement among the islands you may consider working on another island. For details on how, visit **http://www.caricom.org**

4. Because you are also fluent in Spanish and French the entire Caribbean (and the World) is available to you.

5. In a twist of fate you may end up at the college you graduated from. There is nothing to stop you from becoming a lecturer at the Sir Arthur Lewis Community College, or The University of the West Indies.

6. Regionally you may wish to join an agency such as
    a. Caribbean Public Health Agency[1]
    b. Pan American Health Organisation (PAHO)

7. The Nongovernmental Sector (locally, regionally and internationally) also works with Radiologist e.g. Medicine Sans Frontiers.

8. Internationally you may work for the Centre for Disease Control (CDC) in the USA or a UN Agency. United Nations Young Professional Program – targets highly qualified young persons. By this they mean first level university degree, aged 32 or under fluent in English or French. Further details can be obtained from **http://careers.un.org**

6. Other career options:
    a. Research - Your research may be applied to a variety of areas ranging from product development to social policy.
    b. Publish - write articles or books – *publications and presentations are important to disseminate discoveries. The more you publish and present, the better your position, the higher your raise and the greater the chance for promotion.* (Library of Alexandra – 2014)

---

[1]*An amalgam of five Caribbean Regional Health Institutes (RHIs) into a single agency, they are:*

The Caribbean Environmental Health Institute (CEHI)
The Caribbean Epidemiology Centre (CAREC)
The Caribbean Food and Nutrition Institute (CFNI)
The Caribbean Health Research Council (CHRC)
The Caribbean Regional Drug Testing Laboratory (CRDTL)

Professional Development

The Law

In Saint Lucia, Radiologists are governed by the Labour Code and the Health Practitioners Act No. 33 of 2006.

Continuing Professional Development

Continuing professional development (CPD) is the means by which people maintain their knowledge and skills related to their professional lives. You should always keep informed of the new technologies and philosophies of your career.

Professional Associations

Most professions have an umbrella body that keeps members informed of new technologies and philosophies related to the subject matter. Many require that members conduct CPD. There are various categories of membership and many of these professional associations also have a Student Membership category.

Once you graduate you would then change status from student to professional. Depending on where you study and work, as a practicing Radiologist you may be eligible for membership within:
1. SaintLucia Medical and Dental Association - **http://www.slmda.org/**
2. Caribbean Society of Radiologists - **http://www.csor.org/**

Acknowledgements

I would like to thank
- LL for the reading, catching and correcting my spelling and grammar.

Notes

What the Reviewers are saying...

This is an excellent resource for the youth that is worth sharing! – Banker

I thought that the booklet was a welcome contribution for persons searching for more information before pursuing a possibly deeply-entrenched career path. – ICT Specialist

Your series of books – Excellent idea and I am sure will be well received. – Chiropractor

First of all, let me say that I think this is a wonderful service that you are providing for our youth, - Naturopath

I think the book is a necessary tool and can be of great assistance to new entrants to that field; - Diplomat

A very good idea about the series – Diplomat

...this is a most needed and practical book that may be used by most if not all countries in the Caribbean. – Senior Military Officer

This has the potential to be a very interesting and useful book for youth in Saint Lucia and elsewhere. – Communications Expert

Timely, inspiring; wish I had it growing up, would have made better choices. Serious about education and productive futures for our children or the country. Invest in a book.
- Mother of Teenagers

Congratulations on your series of books, I think this is a great idea! – Human Resource Manager

Thanks for bringing out this document. I am truly impressed. Congratulations! – Funeral Home Director

Interesting, very interesting – Funeral Home Director

I think this is a wonderful idea – Firefighter

A masterpiece - Meteorological Officer

We need to customize the world for Saint Lucia…, so go ahead. – Media Manager

I am impressed with the document and keep up the good work. – Musician

As usual this book will be very useful to a lot of people. It was a great eye-opener for me. – Corporate Manager

Good stuff you have doing ... I like it! – ICT Specialist

I would like to commend you again for this. It's a good foundation. – Massage Therapist

I was very impressed when you started discussing the career path for persons with minimum or no qualifications.
– Dental Student

Congratulations on a well put together book! – Photographer

I'm glad you are doing this book. So many people want to become physiotherapists but don't know how. –Physiotherapist

It's very interesting. Just what our youth need. – Inventories Officer

First let me applaud what thus far seems to be a refreshing and easy to understand publication; another in a hopefully long line of inspiring and informative works we can come to expect from you. I wish you the best of luck in completing your mission to educate our young public on the various career paths available to them as I have always lamented the fact that students receive very little exposure to the insurance industry. – Insurance Broker

I think that the idea behind the series is an outstanding one. It is time information on possible work options was put out in plain English for persons trying to make up their minds as to what direction and what is needed to get their foot in the door – EMT

Complimentary Information

Available online at http://tiny.cc/dawnnboooks

A Commonsense Approach to Managing Money
A discussion on the management of money. How to view money as a tool.

A Commonsense Approach to the Job Market
A discussion on tools to use when looking for a job. Common mistakes to avoid

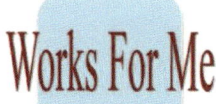

Works for Me: Sales and Marketing
Folks have shown me the way to market my product. Now it is my turn to share what I have been taught.